A Guide to

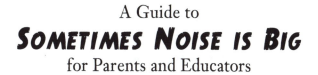

SOMETIMES NOISE IS BIG

for Parents and Educators

by the same author

Sometimes Noise is Big
Life with Autism
Angela Coelho
Illustrated by Camille Robertson
ISBN 978 1 78592 373 9
eISBN 978 1 78450 719 0

of related interest

Can I tell you about Autism?
A guide for friends, family and professionals
Jude Welton
Illustrated by Jane Telford
ISBN 978 1 84905 453 9
eISBN 978 0 85700 829 9

Is It OK to Ask Questions about Autism?
Abi Rawlins
ISBN 978 1 78592 170 4
eISBN 978 1 78450 439 7

A Parents' ABC of the Autism Spectrum
Stephen Heydt
ISBN 978 178592 164 3
eISBN 978 1 78450 435 9

Why Johnny Doesn't Flap
NT is OK!
Clay Morton and Gail Morton
Illustrated by Alex Merry
ISBN 978 1 84905 721 9
eISBN 978 1 78450 190 7

I'll tell you why I can't wear those clothes!
Talking about tactile defensiveness
Noreen O'Sullivan
ISBN 978 1 84905 510 9

A Guide to
SOMETIMES
NOISE IS
BIG
for Parents and
Educators

Angela Coelho and Lori Seeley

Illustrated by Camille Robertson

Jessica Kingsley *Publishers*
London and Philadelphia

First published in 2018
by Jessica Kingsley Publishers
73 Collier Street
London N1 9BE, UK
and
400 Market Street, Suite 400
Philadelphia, PA 19106, USA

www.jkp.com

Library of Congress Cataloging in Publication Data
Names: Coelho, Angela, author. | Seeley, Lori, author. | Robertson, Camille
illustrator.
Title: A guide to sometimes noise is big for parents and educators / Angela
Coelho and Lori Seeley ; illustrated by Camille Robertson.
Description: London ; Philadelphia : Jessica Kingsley Publishers, 2018. |
Audience: Age 5+ | Includes bibliographical references and index.
Identifiers: LCCN 2017022918 | ISBN 9781785923746 (alk. paper)
Subjects: LCSH: Autism in children--Juvenile literature. | Sensory disorders
in children--Juvenile literature. | Sensitivity (Personality
trait)--Juvenile literature.
Classification: LCC RJ506.A9 C58 2018 | DDC 618.92/85882--
dc23 LC record available at https://lccn.loc.gov/2017022918

British Library Cataloguing in Publication Data
A CIP catalogue record for this book is available from the British Library

ISBN 978 1 78592 374 6
eISBN 978 1 78450 720 6

Printed and bound in the United States

To all the parents, caregivers, and educators
who give of themselves daily

CONTENTS

1

...

INTRODUCTION

This guide is intended to be a stepping-off point into the sometimes overwhelming task of understanding autism spectrum disorders (ASDs) and sensory processing challenges. There are many published works written by doctors, psychologists, and professionals—and intended for other professionals—on the topic of ASD, but there is still a gap when it comes to easy-to-read guides that simplify the information, making it accessible to everyone. This guide was written as a companion book to the children's book *Sometimes Noise is Big* to help fill that gap and provide information and strategies for parents, caregivers, and educators. Recommendations for further reading can be found at the end of the book.

2

...

WHAT IS AUTISM?

Autism spectrum disorder is a neurodevelopmental condition that affects the way individuals perceive, respond to, and interact with the world around them. Neurodevelopmental conditions affect the nervous system. In the case of ASD, the brain is the area of the nervous system affected. It can affect social relationships and communication with others.

According to the Centers for Disease Control and Prevention (2017), autism affects approximately 1.4 percent of the population. That statistic is constantly changing as diagnostic procedures improve and become more standard. Increasing public awareness also increases the number of families that seek support for their children with neurological differences.

Children with autism are highly variable in their ability to engage and function. Some children with autism grow to lead independent lives, while others require varying degrees of support, which may change throughout their life. This support may also change as a result of better awareness and accommodations for the unique learning and functional needs of each person with autism.

3
...

SENSORY ISSUES

Many children with autism experience some degree of sensory processing difficulties. Sensory processing disorder (SPD) is common in autistic children, but can be found in other conditions as well. Children with SPD interpret sensory information in a different manner than someone who is considered neurotypical (without autism or SPD). These children may find sensations to be overwhelming and intense, or conversely, their systems may under-respond to sensory information. They may seek out sensations or experience them in a very muted manner, which can affect their ability to understand and attend to the world around them.

It is also important to understand that sensory systems include more than the common five of touch, taste, smell, sight, and hearing. They also include the sense of movement (vestibular sense) and positioning of the body (proprioceptive sense). All of these sensory systems work in concert with one another.

The characters in the children's book *Sometimes Noise is Big* share how their sensory systems are affected. This guide provides additional information about these sensory experiences to help readers understand the experience and identify some beginning strategies to support children with autism who have these challenges.

For some children, their reaction to the sensory environment can lead to the dysregulation of their system in response to sensory overload. These children may have a limited ability to control their emotional and behavioral reactions, as they are in a state similar to fight, flight, or freeze. In this state, children may be unable to respond to direction, and only able to react to their sensory system. They may protect themselves by attempting to run away or withdraw, combat the situation that is causing the distress, or become unresponsive or stuck in place and unable to move or react, even when faced with a dangerous situation.

4

. . .

LIGHT SENSITIVITY

Sometimes when I wake up in the morning, the light is REALLY LOUD and it hurts my eyes.

Some children have a sensitivity to light, and as with all children who experience sensory issues, this sensitivity can range from mild to intense. Others experience a dysregulated system because of the quick transition from a resting to a waking state. Some children benefit from the use of special filters in either optical lenses or colored overlay sheets and lower light settings in the room; these help remove some of the light stimulus. Children who are sensitive to light might squint, lay their heads down and cover their heads with their arms, or vocalize that it is "too bright." Optometrists can provide the most accurate assessment of a child's responsiveness to light-filtering strategies.

Children who are low-sensory responders may need a lot of light in a room to concentrate. They may have a strong interest in bright or moving lights.

To assist the child who is easily overwhelmed by visual stimuli other than light, reduce the number of hanging mobiles, and keep wall spaces reasonably clear. Alternatively, allow one wall to be bare so that the child can direct his or her attention to a clean view. In classroom settings, keep the boards clear except for the material that the student should be focusing on at the moment. Keep in mind that a child staring at a blank space may not be tuning you out; he or she may, in fact, be using that as a strategy to focus better.

5

NOISE SENSITIVITY

Sometimes noise is REALLY BIG, even
when it is small for everyone else.

Changes in the way sound is perceived are common among children with ASD. In some cases, they are hypersensitive to noise. Loud noises may startle ASD children more than their neurotypical peers. Children with hypersensitivity may have difficulty filtering out background noises or focusing on the most important sounds. In addition, certain frequencies of sounds or features of the sound itself—rather than the volume—create discomfort for some children.

Strategies to assist children with noise hypersensitivities include using noise-canceling headphones, earmuffs, or earplugs; quieting learning environments; and reducing hard surfaces in classrooms or common living areas. Providing advance warning for loud noises can also reduce a child's intense reaction. For instance, a child might be able to tolerate the sound of the vacuum cleaner if he or she is prepared for the noise.

Contrary to popular belief, children who are hypersensitive to noise are not always the quietest children in the classroom. Their auditory-processing differences affect how they *perceive* sound, not how they *produce* sound. The unpredictability of sound produced by others is different from the sounds children produce themselves, which they anticipate. Children who are under-responsive to noise may also make noise for noise's sake and seek out activities that produce high levels of sound.

There is a condition known as hyperacusis which can occur in both autistic and neurotypical children. Hyperacusis is defined as a reduced tolerance to everyday environmental sounds. The decreased tolerance to sound is usually noticed with sudden high-pitched noises like alarms, bus brakes, the clattering of silverware and dishes, children's crying, and clapping.

Some older children or young adults with autism have expressed that they often create their own noise or output to counteract the noise input around them that can be overstimulating. If a child is humming, tapping, or creating other noises it is important to not try to stop this behavior, and to offer a body break or options such as headphones to help him or her deal with the overstimulation.

There has been some success with Therapeutic Listening, which involves special music and headphones that help desensitize the brain to hyperacusis and help teach the brain to filter noise on its own. An occupational therapist would be a good resource for tips and further information.

6

...

EMOTIONAL EXPRESSION

Sometimes I am so excited that I need to
SCREAM and run in circles to let it out.

Children with ASD may not have typical ways of expressing intense emotions. Running in circles, making noises instead of speaking words, jumping, and bouncing are just some examples of how these children might express excitement, anxiety, frustration, joy, or other emotions.

Sometimes they may experience difficulty regulating these emotions and may use movement or "stimming" behaviors—repetitive movements, sounds, or actions such as hand flapping, rocking, foot tapping or bouncing, and watching spinning objects—to help themselves calm down.

As children learn other coping strategies, their use of these movements may lessen. Providing structured time or space for these actions may help a child learn to use them as coping strategies when it does not interfere with other activities. Some children also use stimming and movement to create stimulation in their environments or to regulate themselves with predictable sensory input.

A personalized program for the classroom with the help of a behaviorist, occupational therapist, or developmental consultant can help with options to promote self-awareness of when a child needs a break. Break cards that the child has and can quietly hand to a support worker when he or she starts to feel overwhelmed are a great tool. There are also many other programs available through autism support groups that are designed to teach children how to more clearly identify and express their emotions.

OVERWHELMING FEELINGS

Sometimes feelings are SO HUGE, I feel like they are a GIANT WAVE crashing down on me.

Often children with ASD or sensory processing disorders experience sensory input and emotions more intensely than neurotypical individuals. Children may react to this intensity in various ways, and each child may have different strategies to help manage emotions or other overwhelming sensations.

In some children, feeling overwhelmed may increase stimming behaviors or result in meltdowns or shutdowns. Deep pressure applied to the arms or head may be helpful for some children. Some may also benefit from extra physical activity to burn off the excess energy. These strategies can help a child regain a sense of control and calm. Most effective is for parents and caregivers to draw from a variety of strategies that have worked in the past, bearing in mind that children's responses to calming strategies can vary from one time to another.

It is also important to probe and discuss what a child finds calming before he or she hits a highly emotional state. Some children benefit from touch and/or deep pressure, while others can't handle being touched at all when in a heightened emotional state.

TEXTURE SENSITIVITY— CLOTHING

Sometimes my clothes feel ITCHY and HURT my skin, even when they are fine for other people.

It is common for children with ASD to have heightened sensitivity to touch and textures, including clothing. Stitching, a fabric's weave or texture, tags, and zippers can create discomfort. In some cases, this can cause children to avoid or resist wearing clothing altogether.

These sensitivities can interfere with sleep if the fabric texture causes discomfort. Adults are able to appreciate the irritation caused by rough clothing tags, for example. Most neurotypical children become accustomed to this type of sensation and stop noticing it quickly. However, children with sensory processing challenges can continue to have the same intense reaction to that sensation until the offending texture is removed. Their nervous systems cannot filter out the information as no longer relevant, and it can be very distracting.

Adults need to be aware that these unintended and ongoing sensations can greatly interfere with a child's attention to more important things. To better understand this perspective, imagine hiking with a sharp pebble in your boot. Until that pebble is removed, you might be so distracted by your discomfort that you fail to appreciate the beauty that surrounds you.

Parents can help by looking for clothing without tags or embroidery, socks without seams, pull-on pants (trousers) without zippers, and clothing with smooth textures. It is also important for parents and caregivers to know that if children are complaining about their clothing and getting upset they are likely being honest. This can often be mistaken as a behavioral issue, when it is in fact sensory.

FOOD AVERSIONS

Sometimes my mouth doesn't like how food
FEELS, even if it TASTES really good.

As with other sensations described previously, food textures can cause discomfort for some children with ASD or sensory processing challenges. Eating and digestive concerns such as gastrointestinal sensitivities are common in children with ASD. They may avoid foods necessary for balanced nutrition simply because they don't "feel good" in their mouths.

Including a dietician or nutritionist on your team is important if your child has a limited range of preferred foods. Occupational therapists and speech language pathologists can assist with strategies to reduce oral sensitivities and develop a plan to slowly introduce new foods and textures to the eating plan. Without a desensitization plan, continuing to present foods that a child has an adverse reaction to can increase reactive behaviors and discourage your attempts to introduce them and other foods. This can be very frustrating for both parents and the child who struggles with oral sensitivities.

It may also be necessary to cut foods into small pieces and monitor a child closely while he or she is eating due to increased gagging and choking hazards from the sensory reactions. A doctor or nutritionist may also recommend supplements to ensure that the child is getting the required nutrition until he or she can learn to eat a wider range of foods.

While it can appear that a child is being a "fussy eater," the issue is much more complex, and it is common for parents to struggle to get their child with sensory processing challenges to eat a varied diet. Patience from everyone involved and help from the professionals listed above can ease this along.

EYE CONTACT

Sometimes I don't LOOK at you when you are
talking, because I HEAR you better that way.

Many children with ASD are uncomfortable making direct eye contact. Some children have to spend additional energy and concentrate hard to monitor changes in facial expressions and layer nonverbal communication on top of the verbal message. The expressions in someone's face can be too intense, may change too rapidly, or in some cases, may not match the verbal message.

For some children with ASD, it is easier to look away to focus on the words instead of using both sensory pathways. While driving, adults experience a similar sensory phenomenon when they turn down the radio while looking for a street sign or important intersection. One should never assume that children with ASD are not paying attention if they are not maintaining eye contact. If you are unsure if someone with ASD is listening to you, you can simply ask him or her.

Children who struggle with focus when listening may need to sit nearer the teacher in order to help cut out excess noise, or they may require one-to-one direction. Attempting to force eye contact can cause regressions and result in less eye contact. Often children will make eye contact when they feel calm and comfortable and are able to focus, and this is a much easier progression for them.

FOCUS AND OVERSTIMULATION

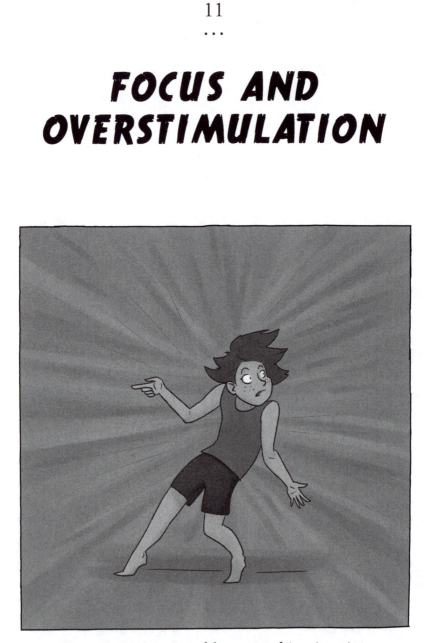

Sometimes it seems like everything is going
SO FAST around me, I can't focus on one thing.

A common theme with children with ASD and sensory processing challenges is that it can be difficult to filter out all the stimuli happening around them. This can overwhelm a nervous system that does not know what to do with all the information coming in at the same time and often at the same intensity. Their system has no way of knowing which sensory information is the most important to pay attention to. This can overwhelm and lead to meltdowns or shutdowns.

Adults can help prevent meltdowns and shutdowns by responding to a child's nonverbal cues when he or she is beginning to become overwhelmed. Moving a child to a quiet, low-stimulation space may allow his or her sensory system time to recover. Providing nonverbal strategies to allow children to express when they are feeling overwhelmed can assist them in learning self-management strategies.

Sometimes verbally expressive children lose their ability to speak when they are overwhelmed. Nonverbal strategies can allow them to get the support they need when they can't ask for help. Each child will have different strategies that work for him or her specifically. It is always important to understand which approaches you can use most successfully in advance of a student experiencing distress. For instance, deep pressure can be very calming for some children, while it can be threatening or uncomfortable for others. Working with a behaviorist to come up with a plan that fits your child can provide strategies that can be employed at home and school, and in other common places your child might visit.

12

...

SELF-REGULATION

Sometimes my world is so BUSY and ALIVE, I
need to sit on my own and shut it out for a while.

While it is true that children with ASD have difficulty with social communication, it would be a mistake to assume that this is always why a child plays independently or sits away from others. Children with ASD expend considerable energy managing the demands of socializing or being in social groups, such as a classroom. Sometimes they seek out spaces away from other children in order to get a break and self-regulate.

Figuring out whether a child is struggling with a social situation or taking a break can be challenging when based only on observation. Asking the child why he or she is sitting off alone can often help an adult figure out what is driving the isolating behavior and lead to creating a plan for responding. A child who plays alone or is isolated may need some coaching on how to join in play with other children, or he or she may need assistance to understand the rules of the game.

It is important for children to have the opportunity to develop skills in both structured and unstructured social situations. If children need time to recover and replenish their energy, strategies can be built into their routines. This respects their need for quiet and alone time, while still creating opportunities to participate with peers, such as at recess.

Often a good approach is to ask children sitting on their own if they are okay and why they are sitting alone. It is also important to watch their body language for upset or to see if they genuinely need some alone time. Awareness of their general socializing behavior also needs to be considered as well.

LINING UP OBJECTS

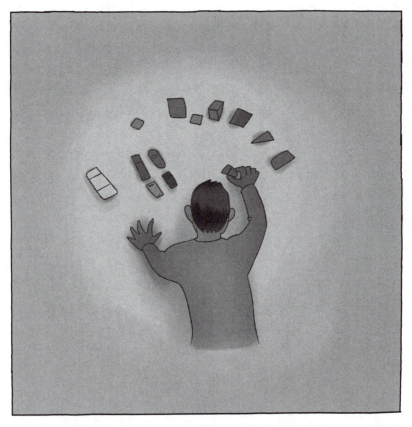

Sometimes I need to put things in ORDER in a way
that makes sense to me, even if you can't see it.

Ordering, sorting, and lining up objects are common activities for many children with ASD. It can be calming and help children feel there is order in their environment. This activity can also help children focus intensely on one activity, allowing them to filter out other stimuli from their environment. In some cases, children can be creating a pattern or structure that others simply can't see or understand yet.

Since these routines can offer comfort and calm to the child with ASD, adults can work within the child's patterns and routines, gradually inserting themselves into the play and adding variations to the routines over time. When a child is highly stressed, these ordering activities can help the child begin to settle a very active nervous system. These activities can also be used to engage the child while expanding his or her play and interactive skills.

LEGO®, KEVA planks, building blocks, train sets with tracks, car tracks and small figurines can give a child a creative outlet to order, sort, and line up objects and it also creates a situation where someone can easily start to interact with the child and insert themselves into the play.

PERSPECTIVE

Sometimes I see things DIFFERENTLY than you,
because I am looking at them from my point of view.

Many children with ASD perceive the world from a different viewpoint than their neurotypical peers. They may see details we overlook, or they may experience things more or less intensely. They may explore and understand objects from a different perspective. For instance, while their neurotypical preschool peers are drawing people with a head, a face, a body, two arms, and two legs, the ASD child may be drawing everything from a bird's-eye view. Not knowing this about the child's drawing might lead one to conclude that his or her drawing skills lack realistic and age-appropriate features.

They may also explore toys in a manner that would be unexpected, such as lying on the ground to view the toy or flipping it over to examine a specific part. They might view the individual parts of a toy with particular interest, while not really attending to the toy as a whole.

Adults can assist a child by commenting on the specific element the child is playing with, mimicking his or her play, and then expanding the play by demonstrating different functions of the toy. This may assist the child in developing the "parts to a whole" understanding.

Many inventors, architects, and other figures throughout history who stood out among their peers are thought, in retrospect, to have been autistic. They often had a perspective and ideas that no one else saw or understood at the time and it was an advantage to them.

MEMORY AND TASKS

Sometimes I can REMEMBER big things
that I have only seen once, and sometimes I
FORGET little things I do every day.

Children with ASD can have highly variable memory skills. In areas of interest, their ability to remember detailed information can be very strong, yet they may lack the ability to demonstrate memory for daily routines and familiar activities. However, what looks like a challenge with memory could also be a challenge with sequencing, being able to initiate an activity, or even motor praxis. (Motor praxis involves all the steps in thinking about what we need to *do*, planning the action, and then carrying out or executing the action.)

Children may struggle to sequence the steps of a daily routine. It can be difficult to support the child's ability to generalize strong memory or sequencing skills from one situation to areas where he or she struggles. Visual charts and other visual cues and reminders can assist the child who struggles with memory, sequencing, motor planning, or even being able to initiate and start an activity.

Utilizing Social Stories™ (Gray, 2015), and adding in subtle, planned variations in teaching and training a child can be helpful. Repetition is important and children with ASD may require more repetitions to learn a skill than their neurotypical peers. Small variations can keep it interesting while still working on the same skill, and may aid in generalizing the task to real-world situations. Patience and perseverance are both very important to the parents and educators in supporting the child.

SPEECH AND COMMUNICATION

Sometimes I SEE the words in my head,
but I can't make them COME OUT.

Struggles to communicate in general or in specific circumstances, such as social interactions, are common in children with ASD. These challenges with communication do not mean that the child lacks the understanding of what is being said to him or her. Fatigue, stress, or overstimulation can all impact the child's ability to verbalize thoughts, even in some children with well-developed speech. Using picture cards or nonverbal gestures can assist the child who is struggling. When children have more extensive communication challenges, teaching basic sign language can offer a means of communication and reduce their stress and frustration.

Not being able to clearly communicate a thought or need is highly stressful for a child with ASD and can result in meltdowns or shutdowns. That is why providing assistance and finding ways to communicate is so important. Personalized emotion cards and pictures can be used at home and in the classroom to help further communication and alleviate stress when a child is trying to communicate a need.

FILTERING SOUNDS

Sometimes it looks like I am NOT LISTENING,
but I HEAR EVERYTHING all around me.

Earlier we talked about how some children with ASD have great difficulty filtering out sounds and focusing on one thing, such as a teacher's voice. This attention to all the sounds around them creates another interesting situation: they can appear to be engaged in their own activity, but they are also taking in all the conversations around them. Some children are not participating directly in the conversation, and yet they uncannily manage to hear what is being said. They may respond to a specific part of the conversation, even though you were convinced they weren't listening to the discussion. Or they might simply act out if what they hear is about them.

This can also explain why a child might be overstimulated or may have missed instructions. It can take a great deal of effort to focus on one individual conversation, rather than trying to filter all the information coming in at once or deciding what is most important.

If you are speaking about a child in front of him or her, it is helpful to assume that the child is a party to that conversation, even though he or she may be playing at a distance away. If the conversation about the child with ASD is of a more private nature, it is best to have the conversation when he or she is not present or to share information in writing. Many parents share that their child can hear from rooms away, even while actively engaged in play or screen time.

PARENT SUPPORT

Sometimes I feel like no one UNDERSTANDS me,
but then you help me just when I need it the most.

Parents and caregivers play a huge role in supporting the child with ASD. Many children with ASD are aware that they are different from other children. Understanding that their behavior is their way of communicating their distress—not a result of deliberate misbehavior—can help guide responses to children that support and encourage them, rather than increase their anxiety. Understanding the responses that are helpful to children when they are upset or stressed can ensure that you assist them, rather than further stress them. Some children respond well to touch and may seek out firm pressure to help calm them. Other children may respond negatively to touch and shrink away from it. Knowing this in advance of stressful situations can help you prepare with an appropriate plan of support.

Some children with ASD experience very high anxiety or stress reactions. Parents and caregivers can best assist them by reassuring them that they are safe and by using a calm tone of voice and relaxing their body position. Mirroring or matching children's level of stress and anxiety may increase the challenges that they have in self-calming.

Adults may not know what is creating the stress reaction in a child. Continuing to make him or her feel safe and protected will help in bringing those stress levels down. When the stress has passed, asking the child about the triggers to the upset—asking about feelings or perspective—can uncover some gems that will help you understand the world from the child's perspective.

Many adults can be discouraged, especially when certain behaviors seem to intensify at home, but this often means that is the child's "safe space" and that the parent just being there is often support in itself.

LITERAL THINKING

Sometimes I do EXACTLY what you SAID,
but not exactly what you ASKED.

Our communication processes are very tricky. We communicate in metaphors, idioms, and colloquialisms, such as slang or language shortcuts. Children with ASD can be very literal in their interpretation of language. "Get off your high horse" would mean something different to most adults than it does to many children with ASD.

Here is another example: A child might be told, "It's time to go to bed." Adults interpret this to mean that the expectation is that the child will get into bed and go to sleep. In the image, the child followed through with the request to go to bed, but the expectation to go to sleep was not explicitly stated, so that part of the instruction was missed.

It is important for adults not to assume misbehavior or manipulation in these situations. Planning out your conversations and your requests and considering how the message might be received can help you communicate clearly what the expectations are.

Children with ASD can learn idioms and colloquialisms, but they often need to be explicitly taught their meaning and use. Teaching language shortcuts can benefit children in their interactions outside of familiar people, but generally it is best to be clear and explicit when communicating with children with ASD.

There are several behavioral programs and even "apps" that are designed to teach these language idioms and slang to children with ASD. A behaviorist, therapist, or child development consultant can help identify which programs might work the best for each child.

SIMILARITIES AND UNIQUENESS

Sometimes I feel like I am DIFFERENT
from everybody else, but then I find
things that are the same too.

Developing a sense of belonging and identity is something that begins with children in infancy (Brooker & Woodhead, 2008). All children have a different awareness of whether they are different from others.

Children with differences that include autism or sensory processing disorders may notice that they do not react the same as other children; they may not understand the world around them the same as others. Helping children develop a positive self-concept may mean assisting them to embrace their differences and how they are unique. Helping children understand both their differences, and what they have in common with others, helps them better relate to others. For instance, in this figure, a child knows that he is different from a peer, but that they are wearing something similar and have a similar interest. This awareness can be expanded into a social conversation. "Hey look, we have the same t-shirt. Red isn't my favorite color, but I like this shirt. What's your favorite color?"

Embracing differences and similarities all adds up to helping to identify our individual uniqueness as being a positive thing. This also helps to move away from the concepts of "normal" and "abnormal" into neurodiversity, which is a healthier view of differences.

HOME BEHAVIORS VERSUS SCHOOL

Sometimes I work so hard to keep myself
CALM all day, just to come home and
let out all my feelings at once.

It is not uncommon for parents of a child with autism, sensory processing disorders, or other neurobehavioral conditions to hear that school staff don't see the kinds of behavior that a parent reports, especially if the student does well in his or her coursework. This is frustrating for parents, who may feel staff are not hearing their concerns. It can impact academic progress or increase anxiety, as the child may not be able to complete homework in the evening. This occurs when the child is too dysregulated to participate in expected activities. Dysregulation is the inability to control emotional responses and can lead to meltdowns.

Reactions to seemingly small events might be much bigger than expected. Children develop skills in hiding these reactions during the day, often because it leads to teasing or disapproval from others. Pushing down these reactions takes a lot of energy. Often by the time they reach home at the end of the day, they have no energy left to manage their feelings and reactions. Even the smallest thing can result in a meltdown. Children may feel that home is the only safe place to release the valve on their pent-up feelings. It can be very helpful for children to have no chores, homework, or even after-school activities for the first hour at the end of a school day. This allows their body and mind some rest, and prepares them for other activities in the evening, or even just helps to take the edge off so reactions are smaller or shorter in duration. We often call this decompression time.

Teachers can assist by reducing or eliminating homework demands. This can either be a choice that is made for all students, or can be an expectation that is built into an individual student's education plan.

TIGHT SPACES

Sometimes I need to be in a TIGHT SPACE.
It helps me feel calm, safe, and relaxed.

When sights, sounds, and other information overwhelm children, they might seek a way to escape. Small spaces sometimes allow a child to shut everything out. It can be surprising to find a child hiding in a cupboard or curled up on a bookcase shelf. Chances are, they feel quite at peace with the idea.

Some children will also seek out spaces that allow them to feel deep pressure, as another way to feel soothed. For instance, some children will hide out between the mattress and the wall, under a pile of heavy blankets, or curled up in a plastic tote. It can be very calming, as long as the weight or pressure is safe and they have the ability to breathe. Deep pressure, also known as proprioceptive input, is very calming to the central nervous system.

Providing a safe and easily accessible option for a child who exhibits this behavior is important for several reasons. First, it allows a safe retreat for the child where he or she can go when needed and will ensure he or she doesn't venture into something potentially harmful. Second, the parent will know where to look for the child instead of having to search any small, tight spaces the child might otherwise seek out. Small forts, therapy swings, or areas cleared in a closet are all great options.

FIGHT, FLIGHT, AND FREEZE

Sometimes all the LIGHT and NOISE
around me is too much to handle, so I scream
and kick or get quiet and don't move.

Constantly trying to filter out sights, sounds, smells, the feel of clothing or the chair, and everything else that's going on can be quite overwhelming. If the child is feeling any frustration over and above all of these things, the reaction can be unexpected. We talked about the fight, flight, or freeze reaction in Chapter 3. When a child is overstimulated by all that is going on around him or her, the child can melt down (fight), bolt (flight), or shut down (freeze). A meltdown is a strong reaction that is generally outside of the child's control and in response to feeling overwhelmed. It can appear as a verbal or physical outburst such as screaming, yelling, lashing out, biting, self-harm, or destroying things.

The most urgent need for a child in the midst of a meltdown is to remove objects that make the area unsafe. However, the best approaches to meltdowns are prepared in advance. Understanding how the child responds to supports during a meltdown is very useful. For instance, some children respond well to deep pressure during the build-up of a meltdown, but may react negatively to any touch when at the height of their reaction. Some children prefer an adult to stay close by and provide brief, reassuring comments. It is best to keep the voice low and neutral. Responding can be a matter of trial and error to learn what works best for each child. Teaching children the language for the strategies you use allows them to provide feedback on the ones they like. For example, deep pressure can be "squeeze hugs" or "squishes." "I like the squeeze hugs best." "No talking."

An overwhelmed child who bolts or runs away needs a safety plan in place to address this behavior. Adults can assist by become skilled at recognizing when the child is beginning to get overwhelmed. Suggesting they take a break, redirecting them to less demanding activities or lower-stimulation environments will help prevent the need to escape. This is also a strategy that can support fewer or less intense meltdowns and shorter shutdowns.

A child who shuts down will likely remain in the environment that is overwhelming, unless given assistance to leave to move to a quiet area. Similar support can be provided to this child as you would for the child who is experiencing a meltdown. The triggers are often the same.

It is important to be aware that a child can react in one of these ways or all of them when overwhelmed. Prepare a game plan for each possibility.

STIMMING

Sometimes I TAP or SNAP my fingers or ROCK
back and forth. It's a way to keep myself calm.

As discussed previously, many children will engage in repetitive movements, sounds, or actions, called stimming. People may be familiar with their own stimming behaviors. Clicking a pen, tapping a foot, or swinging your legs in a too-big chair are all examples of stimming.

Stimming serves a purpose. Autistic children and adults who describe their stimming often share that it helps them focus or tune out other sensory stimuli. It can help them when feeling overwhelmed, or it can give them sensory input that they are craving.

Stimming can be helpful for a child, and it is rarely harmful. Stims that are harmful, such as picking at skin or clothing, should be redirected to allow the child to develop harmless sensory stims. Inappropriate stimming behavior, such as touching one's privates while in a public area, can be redirected to private spaces or replaced with alternate activities such as fidget toys or an activity. The replacement for the behavior depends on the reason for the stimming.

Stims that are disruptive, but not harmful, should not be discouraged, but carers can help the child have an outlet for the stimming at an appropriate time. For instance, if children make loud noises in the classroom while completing desk work, it will be disruptive for those around them. Creating the time and space for them to freely engage in stimming will ensure that their needs for this behavior are still being met.

Sit disks, chair bands to quietly kick against, silicone "chew" pencil toppers or necklaces, or exercise ball chairs are often effective in the classroom. Manipulatives, or fidget toys, as they are commonly called, are also an option for children who need that level of stimulation in order to focus. Fidgets, or other tools, that are kinesthetic in nature, can be organizing to the central nervous system. Even adult learning principles suggest that adults pay better attention to verbal teaching strategies if they are given manipulatives or are permitted to doodle or color during presentations (Rotz & Wright, 2005).

As with all tools such as this, boundaries around how the objects may be used in the classroom setting will ensure that they do not become a distraction to other learners. A behaviorist, therapist, or child development consultant can help identify which items might be the most effective for each individual child.

25

SOCIAL INTERACTIONS

Sometimes I want to go and make
FRIENDS with other kids, but I don't
always know what to do and need help.

The reason autistic children struggle with social situations is complex. Autism is a social communication disorder, and it is challenging for children to read and interpret social situations. Some children process the information from social situations more slowly and can't keep up with their peers, or the changes in the play, leaving them often on the outside. Some autistic children are seen as different or "weird," and breaking into a social circle with this label can be difficult.

Autistic children often need to be coached on how to join in play, or how to approach another child. They need information about how to read what a group is doing, how to mimic the play that the other child is doing, and then how to enter that play, without changing the direction of the play and frustrating their play partners. Coaching also provides the opportunity to give the child feedback on what worked when he or she tried to join in and what did not.

Some children need information about what to expect when they join a game with another. What are the rules and how do I play this game? What should happen if someone doesn't follow the rules? What should I do if someone changes the whole game? What should I do if I get overwhelmed during the game?

On the flip side, adults can help teach neurotypical children how to include children who play differently. They can teach them how to notice and invite others into their play and how to make the play inclusive and accessible for kids with differing abilities.

It is also important to remember that some children with ASD will resist a task that is hard for them, such as socializing, and might need strong encouragement. They might claim that they don't want to be social or that they are "introverts." Learning to socialize effectively is a life skill which they will need more and more as they get older and, it is hoped, move into being more independent.

26

LEARNING METHODS

Sometimes you have to SLOWLY SHOW
me how to do something for me to learn it.
TELLING me doesn't always work.

Processing language can be challenging for many children. If a child is filtering many different kinds of information, it may be difficult to attend to instruction that is only verbal. It may also be difficult for children to understand the information you are sharing if they don't make a real connection to the context for that information. For children with autism, and even for those with other processing challenges, using visual cues, hands-on demonstrations, and real-life practice will aid in learning.

The progressive teaching strategy of tell me, show me, involve me does apply here, but placing an emphasis on visuals and hands-on learning will be a stronger approach. Any opportunity for multiple ways of learning (visual, auditory, and kinesthetic/touch/movement) will support children who have challenges processing information through one or more sensory channels. Autistic children more commonly have challenges with auditory processing or slower processing of auditory information (Stewart et al., 2016). This does not mean that they don't understand, but they may need another way to get to that understanding.

It may be necessary to further break down instructions and mirror them slowly for a child to process and track what's being explained.

27

PROBLEM-SOLVING PERSPECTIVES

Sometimes I see a DIFFERENT way to do what you are asking me to, it doesn't mean I'm not listening to you.

Autistic children often see the world from a different perspective than the neurotypical people around them. Often, when asked, autistic children cannot fully explain how they solved a difficult mathematical problem, or their problem-solving process is different to how it's normally taught, yet they come to the same answer. In this figure, the child has probably not responded right away to the parent's request for help, because he is off to find a new tool to deal with the problem. Without pausing to ask or understand why the child is not responding as expected, we might miss the strength of his or her perspective and we may miss the opportunity to share a creative approach to a situation.

While it can be frustrating in home and school situations when a child does not respond as expected, it is important for us to remember that many of the world's innovations came by approaching an old problem from a new angle.

28

SINGULAR INTERESTS

Sometimes I get SO EXCITED about something
that it is ALL I talk about. I am just excited about
what I like and am trying to SHARE it with you.

Autistic children often have special, and sometimes obsessive, interests. These interests can be unusual for their age, or can be in greater intensity than would be expected for a child their age. Their interest may be so strong that it prevents them from having a balanced conversation where the other conversation partner is able to talk about the interest and share their own information.

Parents and educators can assist children by supporting them to be balanced communicators, and cuing them to ask the other person about his or her interests or sharing his or her own experience with the same interest. Special interests can be included in a child's learning and development plan. Engaging a child in an academic task that is difficult can be more motivating if his or her favorite thing becomes part of the assignment.

29

STRENGTHS AND WEAKNESSES

Sometimes I wish people would see all the things
I can do WELL, instead of just what I can't do.

All children have varying abilities and skills, whether a child with autism or a child with neurotypical development. Often when a child has an identified challenge, the conversations become focused on the challenges. If the focus remains on the challenge, the opportunity to recognize and build on strengths can be lost.

While it is not the case with all children with autism, many autistic children have unique abilities. These abilities cannot only be celebrated, but they can often also be redirected to support them to creatively overcome or reduce their challenges. Learning can be channeled to allow them to move in the direction of their strength. Both educators and parents can help nurture the child's strengths by ensuring that learning and care plans identify strengths and ways to leverage them in areas for growth. Where children have ongoing challenges in all areas of development, it is important to celebrate the successes and continue to positively encourage them in their achievements and development.

30

SHOWING LOVE

Sometimes I forget to say, "I LOVE YOU,"
but I try to show you in my own ways.

Verbally expressing emotions can be hard for some children with ASD. They may not feel comfortable expressing themselves. Alternately, they may not see the importance in using words to express how they feel. Some children may not have the language ability to express themselves verbally; just as adults do not always verbally say I love you, children may express this in other ways.

Adults may demonstrate love and caring by preparing morning coffee for a loved one, asking about someone's day, or sharing their excitement about a new project. Children may share their love by drawing a family picture expressing how they feel, approaching a trusted adult to make contact briefly, and then returning to their play, or jumping with excitement at your show of affection. To the child, this is the same as using the words "I love you." Parents often long for this verbal confirmation, but it is important to look for nonverbal ways the child might express this.

Some children with ASD find constantly repeating what they perceive to be a known fact (that they love a parent in this example) to be illogical. Learning perspective outside of themselves and helping them to understand certain social expectations will help them to understand better why some people might want to repeatedly hear certain things, such as "I love you," more often.

31

...

CONCLUSION

In *Sometimes Noise is Big*, we saw many autistic children demonstrate their uniqueness in how they experience the world and communicate with others. Through thoughtful planning, we can increase the opportunities for autistic individuals to participate in the world around them. Attending to things in the environment around autistic children allows all of us to better understand what might be interfering with their ability to be fully present. Understanding the impact of the sensory world and their way of communicating can open many doors to allow these children to feel included, safe, and welcomed.

COMMON ACRONYMS AND TERMS

It is important to note that terminology varies from country to country. Attempts have been made to remove regional references, wherever possible.

ABA (Applied Behavior Analysis/Applied Behavioral Analysis) The process of systematically *applying* principles of behavior and learning theory for the purpose of improving behaviors (Baer, Wolf, & Risley, 1968).

ABC (Autism Behavior Checklist) A series of questions, completed by a parent, caregiver, or teacher, which is primarily used as a screening tool. A trained professional analyzes the results and this information is used in conjunction with other standardized assessments and clinical observations to make a diagnosis of autism spectrum disorder (Volkmar et al., 1988).

ADHD (attention deficit hyperactivity disorder) A neuro-developmental disorder that is characterized by inattention, hyperactivity, and impulsivity to a degree that interferes with function and persists across settings (Polanczyk et al., 2014).

ADOS-2 (Autism Diagnostic Observation Schedule) A standardized observational tool that is used in the assessment and diagnosis of autism for children from age 12 months through adulthood (Lord et al., 2012).

APD (auditory processing disorder) Also known as *central auditory processing disorder* (CAPD). This is a problem that affects about 5 percent of school-aged children. Children with this condition can hear a full range of sounds, but their nervous system does not process and interpret auditory stimuli effectively (Musiek & Chermak, 2013).

AS (Asperger's syndrome) A previously classified subtype of autism spectrum disorder characterized by deficits in social functioning, and patterns of repetitive and stereotyped behavior, interests, and activities. Language delays were not considered a clinically significant feature of Asperger's syndrome (American Psychiatric Association, 1994). With the release of the *Diagnostic and Statistical Manual of Mental Disorders, Fifth Edition* (DSM-5), the condition was folded into the broader autism spectrum disorder diagnosis in 2013.

ASC (autism spectrum condition) Another term for autism spectrum disorder, though not a formally recognized term for diagnostic purposes.

Body break A sensory break from either the classroom or a situation that might be causing overstimulation. This could be walking or other physical outlets such as jumping or exercising, or spending quiet time in a green space.

CDD (childhood disintegrative disorder) Also known as Heller's syndrome, this is a subset of autism spectrum disorder, in which severe autism is developed following regression (Westphal & Le Maistre, 2015).

DCD (developmental coordination disorder) Also commonly referred to as dyspraxia. It is a condition that affects fine and gross motor coordination and spatial relations, or moving the body around objects in the environment. Dyspraxia can impact all aspects of daily living, including dressing, hygiene, writing, and movement in general. Dyspraxia can also be developed following a neurological injury later in life, but this form of dyspraxia is not associated with developmental coordination disorder.

DSM-5 The *Diagnostic and Statistical Manual of Mental Disorders* is used to diagnose and classify mental disorders. This current edition classifies all subtypes of autism under the diagnosis of autism spectrum disorder (American Psychiatric Association, 2013).

Dyscalculia Specific difficulty with mathematical ability, time, and spatial reasoning (Szucs et al., 2013).

Dyslexia A processing difference impacting literacy which creates challenges in reading, writing, and spelling, as well as in cognitive functions such as organization, processing speed, or memory (Reid, 2016).

GFCF Gluten free/casein free: a specific dietary requirement associated with a number of autistic people's digestive systems.

Neurodiversity An approach that argues that diverse neurological conditions are a result of natural cognitive variations and are important to the evolution of technology and our modern world. It was a concept first presented by Hans Asperger in the 1930s (Silberman, 2015).

NOS Not otherwise specified: usually seen in PDD-NOS, a condition detailed in the DSM-IV.

NT Neurologically typical/neurotypical (no diagnosable neurological disorder).

NVLD Nonverbal learning disorder is a learning disability associated with a gap between spatial and verbal intelligence, low visual spatial ability, and decreased social-emotional awareness.

OCD (obsessive compulsive disorder) Unwanted, intrusive thoughts, or repetitive actions intended to reduce anxiety associated with obsessive thoughts (American Psychiatric Association, 2013).

ODD (oppositional defiant disorder) A pattern of disobedient, hostile, and aggressive behavior, often in response to authority figures (American Psychiatric Association, 2013).

OT (occupational therapist/occupational therapy) Promotes health and well-being through "occupation" or activity. The goal of occupational therapy is to support people to participate in everyday life.

PDA (pathological demand avoidance) This describes children with ASD who avoid or resist everyday tasks, often using manipulative, socially inappropriate, sometimes socially shocking behavior (O'nions et al., 2014).

PDD (pervasive developmental disorder) A delay in social, communication, and motor skills.

PDD-NOS (pervasive developmental disorder not otherwise specified) Although previously a distinct diagnosis within the autism spectrum disorders, this condition has been fully folded into autism spectrum disorder in the DSM-5. It was considered a subtype of autism, where the individual was assessed to be on the autism spectrum but did not meet the criteria of autism or Asperger's syndrome.

RHLD (right hemisphere learning disorder) A less common reference to nonverbal learning disorder.

SIB (self-injurious behavior) Also known as self-harm; defined as repetitive, impulsive, and non-lethal harming to oneself. In children with ASD, it can be in response to sensory seeking, high anxiety, or sensory overload.

Social (pragmatic) communication disorder A new diagnostic category in the DSM-5 characterized by deficits in verbal and nonverbal communication, but cannot be diagnosed in conjunction with ASD (American Psychiatric Association, 2013).

SPD (sensory processing disorder) Difficulty with sensory processing, interpreting sensory input, and creating a meaningful response to sensory information. It can cross one or all sensory domains (Miller, Fuller, & Roetenberg, 2014).

Stimming Behavior done to self-soothe or fulfill sensory needs; can include rocking, humming, tapping, snapping, and vocalizing.

Theory of Mind The ability to make inferences and understand that others have thoughts, feelings, and desires that are different from your own (Sodian & Kristen, 2010).

TS (Tourette's syndrome) Sudden involuntary movements or "tics" with vocal noises or inappropriate sounds which cannot be controlled.

REFERENCES

American Psychiatric Association (1994). *Diagnostic and Statistical Manual of Mental Disorders, Fourth Edition (DSM-IV).* Washington, DC: American Psychiatric Association.

American Psychiatric Association (2013). *Diagnostic and Statistical Manual of Mental Disorders, Fifth Edition (DSM-5).* Washington, DC: American Psychiatric Association.

Baer, D. M., Wolf, M. M., & Risley, T. R. (1968). Some current dimensions of applied behavior analysis. *Journal of Applied Behavior Analysis, 1*(1), 91–97.

Brooker, L. & Woodhead, M. (eds) (2008). *Developing Positive Identities: Diversity and Young Children.* Early Childhood in Focus 3. Milton Keynes: Open University.

Centers for Disease Control and Prevention (2017). Autism Spectrum Disorder (ASD): Data and Statistics. Available at https://www.cdc.gov/ncbddd/autism/data.html, accessed on 11 August 2017.

Gray, C. (2015) *The New Social Story Book, Revised and Expanded 15th Anniversary Edition.* Arlington, TX: Future Horizons Incorporated.

Lord, C., Rutter, M., DiLavore, P. C., Risi, S., & Gotham, K. (2012). *Autism Diagnostic Observation Schedule, Second Edition: ADOS-2.* Torrence, CA: Western Psychological Services.

Miller, L. J., Fuller, D. A., & Roetenberg, J. (2014). *Sensational Kids: Hope and Help for Children with Sensory Processing Disorder (SPD), revised edition.* New York: Penguin.

Musiek, F. E., & Chermak, G. D. (eds) (2013). *Handbook of Central Auditory Processing Disorder, Volume I: Auditory Neuroscience and Diagnosis.* San Diego, CA: Plural Publishing.

O'nions, E., Christie, P., Gould, J., Viding, E., & Happé, F. (2014). Development of the "Extreme Demand Avoidance Questionnaire" (EDA-Q): preliminary observations on a trait measure for Pathological Demand Avoidance. *Journal of Child Psychology and Psychiatry, 55*(7), 758–768.

Polanczyk, G. V., Willcutt, E. G., Salum, G. A., Kieling, C., & Rohde, L. A. (2014). ADHD prevalence estimates across three decades: An updated systematic review and meta-regression analysis. *International Journal of Epidemiology, 43*(2), 434–442.

Reid, G. (2016). *Dyslexia: A Practitioner's Handbook.* Chichester: John Wiley & Sons.

Rotz, R., & Wright, S. D. (2005). *Fidget to Focus: Outwit Your Boredom: Sensory Strategies for Living with ADD.* Lincoln, NE: iUniverse.

Silberman, S. (2015). *Neurotribes: The Legacy of Autism and the Future of Neurodiversity.* London: Penguin.

Sodian, B., & Kristen, S. (2010). Theory of Mind. In B. M. Glatzeder, V. Goel, & A. von Müller (eds) *Towards a Theory of Thinking: Building Blocks for a Conceptual Framework.* London: Springer Berlin Heidelberg.

Stewart, C. R., Sanchez, S. S., Grenesko, E. L., Brown, C. M., Chen, C. P., Keehn, B., et al. (2016). Sensory symptoms and processing of nonverbal auditory and visual stimuli in children with autism spectrum disorder. *Journal of Autism and Developmental Disorders, 46*(5), 1590–1601.

Szucs, D., Devine, A., Soltesz, F., Nobes, A., & Gabriel, F. (2013). Developmental dyscalculia is related to visuo-spatial memory and inhibition impairment. *Cortex, 49*(10), 2674–2688.

Volkmar, F. R., Cicchetti, D. V., Dykens, E., Sparrow, S. S., Leckman, J. F., & Cohen, D. J. (1988). An evaluation of the autism behavior checklist. *Journal of Autism and Developmental Disorders, 18*(1), 81–97.

Westphal, A., & Le Maistre, E. (2015). Childhood Disintegrative Disorder. In H. S. Friedman (ed.) *Encyclopedia of Mental Health*, second edition. Oxford: Academic Press.

FURTHER READING

Biel, L., & Peske, N. K. (2005). *Raising a Sensory Smart Child: The Definitive Handbook for Helping Your Child with Sensory Integration Issues*. New York: Penguin.

Buron, K. D. (2006). *When My Worries Get Too Big!: A Relaxation Book for Children Who Live with Anxiety*. Lenexa, KS: AAPC Publishing.

Chara, K. A., & Chara, P. J. (2004). *Sensory Smarts: A Book for Kids with ADHD or Autism Spectrum Disorders Struggling With Sensory Integration Problems*. London: Jessica Kingsley Publishers.

Higashida, N. (2013). *The Reason I Jump: The Inner Voice of a Thirteen-Year-Old Boy with Autism*. New York: Random House.

Jackson, L. (2002). *Freaks, Geeks and Asperger Syndrome: A User Guide to Adolescence*. London: Jessica Kingsley Publishers.

Kranowitz, C. S. (2005). *The Out-Of-Sync Child: Recognizing and Coping with Sensory Processing Disorder*. New York: Penguin.

Moyes, R. A. (2010). *Building Sensory Friendly Classrooms to Support Children with Challenging Behaviors: Implementing Data Driven Strategies!* Arlington, TX: Sensory World.

Nason, B. (2014). *The Autism Discussion Page on Anxiety, Behavior, School, and Parenting Strategies: A Toolbox for Helping Children with Autism Feel Safe, Accepted, and Competent*. London: Jessica Kingsley Publishers.

Rosa, S. (2011). *Thinking Person's Guide to Autism: What You Really Need to Know About Autism, from Autistics, Parents, and Professionals*. Redwood City, CA: Deadwood City Publishing.

Shanker, S. (2013). *Calm, Alert, and Learning: Classroom Strategies for Self-Regulation*. Ontario: Pearson.

INDEX